SMALL HOLDINGS IN INDIA AND THEIR REMEDIES

MAVEN BOOKS

SMALL HOLDINGS IN INDIA AND THEIR REMEDIES

Dr. B. R. AMBEDKAR

MAVEN BOOKS

Chennai   Trichy   Tirunelveli   New Delhi

MAVEN BOOKS

An Imprint of MJP Publishers

ISBN 978-93-88191-94-4   **Maven Books**

All rights reserved   No. 44, Nallathambi Street,
Printed and bound in India   Triplicane, Chennai 600 005

MJP 732   © Publishers, 2018

Publisher   C. Janarthanan

Publisher's Note

The legacy of a country is in its varied cultural heritage, historical literature, developments in the field of economy and science. The top nations in the world are competing in the field of science, economy and literature. This vast legacy has to be conserved and documented so that it can be bestowed to the future generation. The knowledge of this legacy is slowly getting perished in the present generation due to lack of documentation.

Keeping this in mind, the concern with retrospective acquiring of rare books has been accented recently by the burgeoning reprint industry. Maven Books is gratified to retrieve the rare collections with a view to bring back those books that were landmarks in their time.

In this effort, a series of rare books would be republished under the banner, "Maven Books". The books in the reprint series have been carefully selected for their contemporary usefulness as well as their historical importance within the intellectual. We reconstruct the book with slight enhancements made for better presentation, without affecting the contents of the original edition.

Most of the works selected for republishing covers a huge range of subjects, from history to anthropology. We believe this reprint edition will be a service to the numerous researchers and practitioners active in this fascinating field. We allow readers to experience the wonder of peering into a scholarly work of the highest order and seminal significance.

Maven Books

Contents

I

IMPORTANCE OF AGRICULTURE

A study of the economic ways of getting a living will ever remain important These ways generally take the form of industries or services. Confining ourselves to industries, they may be divided into primary and secondary. The primary industries are concerned with extracting useful material from the earth, the soil or water and take the form of hunting, fishing, stock raising, lumbering and mining. These primary or extractive industries are fundamental in two ways: (1) They extract from the physical world useful materials which become the original sources of man's subsistence. (2) They provide raw materials for the secondary or manufacturing industries, for, manufactures, in the language of Dr. Franklin, are simply, "substance metamorphosed". From a national point of view as well, the importance of primary industries is beyond question. But important as are the primary industries, fanning is by far the most important of them all. It is most ancient and abiding of all industries, primary or secondary : while the fact that it is concerned with 'the production of food is enough to make its problems demand our most serious thought. But when a country, like India, depends almost wholly upon farming its importance cannot be exaggerated. The problems of agricultural economy dealing directly with agricultural production are what to produce, the proper proportion of the factors of production, the size of holdings, the tenures of land etc. In this paper it is attempted to deal only with the problem of the size of holdings as it affects the productivity of agriculture.

II

SMALL HOLDINGS IN INDIA

It may be said that some countries are predominantly countries of small holdings while in others it is the large holdings that prevail. According to Adam Smith it is the adoption of the law of primogeniture chiefly due to the exigencies of a military life that leads to the creation and preservation of large holdings. While it is the adoption of the law of equal sub-division necessitated by the comparatively peaceful career of a nation that gives rise to small holdings. He says:—

"When land like moveables is considered as the means only of subsistence and enjoyment, the natural law of succession divides it like them among all the children of the family; of all of whom the subsistence and enjoyment may be supposed equally dear to the father, [thus tending to have small holdings. But when land was considered as the means, not of subsistence merely, but of power and protection it was thought better that it should descend undivided to one. In those disorderly times.......to divide it was to ruin it, and to expose every part of it to be opposed and swallowed up by its neighbors. The law of primogeniture, therefore came to take place in the succession of landed estates [thus tending to preserve large holdings][1]

England is, therefore, a country of large holdings. Post-Revolutionary France is a country of small holdings. So are Holland and

[1]   Wealth of Nations. BK. III Ch. 11.

Denmark. Turning to India, we find holdings of the following size held separate and direct for the years 1896-97 and 1900-01:

Average area of holdings in acres

Years	Assam	Bombay	Central Provinces	Madras
1896-97	3.37	24.07	17	7
1900-01	3.02	23.9	48	7

Data, more recent, more exact, though from more restricted area, is available from the Baroda State.[2] Statistics of land holdings in the State are summarized in bighas in the following table:[3]

Name of the District	Total Agri cultural land	Survey No. into which it is divided	Number of Khate dars	Average under Khatedar	Average area per Survey No.
Baroda	17,17,319	4,30,601	107,638	15—19—2	4
Kadi	25,13,982	5,89,687	141,145	17—16—5	4 1/4
Naosari	10,46,176	2,16,748	52',652	19—17—8	4
Amveli	9,72,040	55,635	17,214	36—9—7	3 1/4
Total ..	82,49,517	12,92,671	318,649	17—10-10	3 7/8

(8 bighas = = 5 acres)

Another investigation conducted by Dr. H. S. Mann and his colleagues indicates more specifically the fact of small holdings in the village of Pimpala Saudagar near Poona. The size of holdings in that village is indicated by the table below:[4]

---

2 Report of the Committee appointed to make proposals on the Consolidation of Small and Scattered holdings in the Baroda State, 1917. This will be throughout referred to as R.B.C.

3 ibid., p. 3

4 Land and Labour in a Deccan Village 1927, p. 48.

	Over 20 acres	10 to 20 acres	5 to 10 acres	3 to 5 acres	2 to 3 acres	1 to 2 acres	30 to 40 gunthas	20 to 30 gunthas	15 to 20 gunthas	10 to 15 gunthas	5 to 10 gunthas	Below 5 gunthas
Number of plots of each size.	1	7	21	25	67	164	75	136	71	57	59	25

(40 Gunthas= =1 acre)

In this table the modal holding is between 1 and 2 acres. A mode is a statistical average indicating the point of largest frequency in an array of instances.

From these tables it can be easily seen that the average size of holdings varies from 25.9 acres in the Bombay Presidency to an acre or two in Pimpala Saudagar.

This diminutive size of holdings is said to be greatly harmful to Indian Agriculture. The evils of small holdings no doubt, are many. But it would have been no slight mitigation of them if the small holdings were compact holdings. Unfortunately they are not. A holding of a farmer though compact for purposes of revenue is for purposes of tillage composed of various small strips of land scattered all over the village and interspersed by those belonging to others. How the fields are scattered can only be shown graphically by a map. Herein we shall have to remain content, since we cannot give a map, with knowing how many separate plots are contained in aholding. The number of separate plots in each holding will show how greatly fragmented it is. We have no figures at all for the whole of India bearing on this aspect of the question. But the Hon'ble Mr. G. F. Keatinge in his note[5] submitted to Government in 1916 has collected figures of typical cases from all the districts of the Bombay Presidency. The following table is constructed to present his data in an intelligible form :

---

5   The author is thankful to him for a copy of this valuable note.

Case II		Case V		Case VI		Case VII		Case IX		Case X		Case XII	
V. Shirgaon		V. Badlapur		V. Kara		V. Althan		Surat		Kaira		V. Lhasurna	
T. Ratnagiri		T. Kalyan		T. Mawal		T. Ghorssi		District		District		T. Koregaon	
D. Ratnagiri		D. Thana		D. Poona		D. Surat						D. Satara	
Area of holding	No. of separaten plots	Area of a holding	No. of separate plots	Area of a holding	No. of separate plots	Area of a holding	No. of saparate plots	Area of a holding	No. of separate plots	Area of a holding	No.of rate plots	Area of a holding	No.of separate plots
A. g		A g.		A. g.		A. g.		A. g.		A. g.		A. g	
341/2	3	48 6	53	60 0	27	0	9	1 0	14	62 13	27	38	6
33	2	67 0	38	2 27	8	85 0	8	13 0	18	65	23	23	7
20.	3	1 9	6	2 31	5	26 9	8	22 0	20	36 16	16	36	3
1 14	3	6 30	8	16 6	7	..		3 6	4	7 9	5	22	10
1 30	5	24 0	17	2 35	6			5 0	7	5 26	5		..
1 101	4							1 26	9	13 16	6		..
6 33	9							0 26	9	28 4	15		..

Case II		Case V		Case VI		Case VII		Case IX		Case X		Case XII	
V. Shirgaon		V. Badlapur		V. Kara		V. Althan		Surat		Kaira		V. Lhasurna	
T. Ratnagiri		T. Kalyan		T. Mawal		T. Ghorssi		District		District		T. Koregaon	
D. Ratnagiri		D. Thana		D. Poona		D. Surat						D. Satara	
Area of hold ing	No. of sepa- raten plots	Area of a hold ing	No. of sepa- rate plots	Area of a hold ing	No. of sepa- rate plots	Area of a hold ing	No. of sapa- rate plots	Area of a hold ing	No. of sepa- rate plots	Area of a hold ing	No.of rate plots	Area of a hold- ing	No.of sepa- rate plots
3 29 1/2	7									12 10	8		
2 20 1/2	1		..						..	12 7	3		
353/4	3	..								5 26	5		
										3 34	5		..
			..							3 39	3		..

(A- = = acre g = = guntha V = = village taluka D = = district)

These small and scattered holdings have given a real cause for anxiety regarding our great national industry. Comparative Statistics go to swell this feeling by laying bare two very noteworthy but equally sad facts regarding economic life in India ; (1) that it is largely an agricultural country ;* and (2) that its agricultural productivity is the lowest :—

(1) Occupational Statistics

Percentage of Agricultural Population

England and Wales	15.3
Australia	44.7
Belgium	60.9
Bulgaria	20.7
Denmark	82.6
Denmark	48.2
France	42.7
Germany	35.2
Holland	30.7
Hungary	69.7
Italy	59.4
Russia	58.3
Russia	30.9
India	71.5
USA	33.3

(2) Produce in Lbs. per acre

Country	Wheat	Maize
UK	1973	
Canada	1054	3487
New Zealand	1723	3191
Austria	1150	1135
Egypt	1634	2059
France	1172	1097
Germany	1796	-
Hungary	1056	1489
Japan	1176	1525
USA		
Turkey	1318	1372
Indian Provinces		
UP	850	1100
NWP	555	735
Punjab	555	766
Bombay	510	
U. Burma	322	

Both these truths are painful enough to have startled many people into inquiring the causes of this low productivity. As a result, attention has now been concentrated on the excessive sub-division and fragmentation of agricultural holdings. Enlarge and consolidate the holdings, it is confidently argued, and the increase in agricultural productivity will follow in its wake !!

III

CONSOLIDATION

Consolidation of holdings is a practical problem while the enlargement of them is a theoretical one, demanding a discussion of the principle which can be said to govern their size. Postponing the consideration of the theoretical question of enlargement, we find that the problem of consolidation raises the following two issues:—(1) how to unite such small and scattered holdings as the existing ones, and (2) once consolidated how to perpetuate them at that size. Let us consider them each in turn. Sub-division of land need not involve what is called the fragmentation of land. But unfortunately it does, for, every heir desires to secure a share from each of the survey numbers composing the entire lands of the deceased instead of so arranging the distribution that each may get as many whole numbers as possible, i.e. the heirs instead of sharing the lands by survey numbers, claim to share in each survey number, thus causing fragmentation. Though fragmentation does subserve the ends of distributive justice it renders farming in India considerably inefficient as it once did in Europe. It involves waste of labour and cattle power, waste in hedges and boundary marks, and waste of manure. It renders impracticable the watching of crops, sinking of wells and the use of labour saving implements. It makes difficult changes in cultivation, the making of roads, water channels, etc., and it increases the cost of production. These disadvantages of fragmentation arc I to be recounted only to lend their support to the process of restripping or \ consolidation. The methods of "restripping" are many, though all are not equally efficacious. Voluntary exchanges can hardly be relied upon for much. But a restricted sale of the right of occupancy may be expected to go a good deal. For, under it, when survey numbers are put to auction on account of their being relinquished by the holders or taken in attachment for arrears of assessments, only those may be allowed lo bid in the auction for the sale of the right of occupancy whose lands are contiguous to the land hammered out. Again as further helping the process of reunion, the right of pre-emption may be given to farmers whose neighbour wishes to sell his land. These methods, it must be admitted, can achieve the desired result in a very small measure. The evils of fragmentation are very great and must be met by a comprehensive scheme of consolidation. It is, therefore, advocated[6] that if two-thirds of the Khatedars, dealing more than half of the village lands, apply, Government, should undertake compulsorily to restrip the scattered fields of the village. This compulsory restripping is to be executed on two principles, (1) of "Economic Unit" and (2) of "Original Ownership". Regarding the merits of these two principles the Baroda Committee observes.[7]

"In the first the value of each holding is ascertained, then the original boundaries are removed, roads are marked out, lands required for public purposes are set apart, and the rest of the land is parcelled out into new plots. Each of these new plots must be of such a size as, having regard to the local conditions of soil, tillage etc. to form an economic field, i.e., a parcel of land necessary to keep fully engaged and support one family. These new plots may be sold by auction among the old occupants, restriction being placed on purchase so as to prevent a large number of cultivators

6   RBC, p. 35.

7   R. B.C., p. 38

from being ousted. The purchase money may then be divided in a certain proportion among the original owners of pieces, a portion being reserved for expenses, in which Government would also contribute a share. Another mode would be to acquire all the land of the village then to sell it in newly constituted plots by auction as is done by City Improvement Trusts or by Government when laying out new roads in Cities or when extending a town. But we do not recommend its adoption in the improvement of agricultural land. It may result in land speculation and the small holders may be ousted in such numbers as to cause a real hardship.

"According to the second method when the restripping has been decided, a list of Khatedars and their holdings is made and the latter are valued at their market price by Panchas. Then the land is redistributed and each Khatedar is given new land in proportion to his original holding and as far as possible of the same value, difference to be adjusted by cash payment. In this method no Khatedar is deprived of his land. Each is accommodated and in the place of his original small and scattered fields gets one plot of almost their aggregate size. It is only a few people whose holding may be very small and whom it would not be expedient to keep on as farmers, that may have to lose their small pieces. But they too would benefit as they would get their full value in money."

The Baroda Committee prefers the second method because:

"It takes as its starting principle, that nobody (except perhaps a few, holding plots of insignificant sizes) is going to be driven off the land. It will give even the smallest man, chance to better his condition. Each land holder receives a new compact piece of land proportionate to the value of his old small and scattered field. In this way the previous sub-divisions together with their attendant evils totally disappear."[8] Regarding consolidation Prof. H. S. Jevons says:

"The principles which should guide the choice of a method of carrying out the re-organization of villages on the lines above described are the following. In the first place compulsion should be avoided as far as possible and the principle adopted that no charge should be imposed upon any area unless the owners of more than one-half of that area desire the change. Should this condition be satisfied for an area......... it would seem expedient that legal power should be taken to compel the minority to accept the redistribution of holdings under the supervision of Government. In the second place............the expense of the operation should be kept as low as possible.........In the third place considerable elasticity should be permitted in the methods of carrying through the re-organization in the different places during the first few years, as the whole undertaking would be in an experimental stage so that different methods might be tried, and the best be ultimately selected for a permanent set of regulations. Fourthly, the possible necessity for a considerable change of the existing tenancy law in the re-organised villages must be faced............ For the sake of completeness I may add as a fifth principle the obvious condition that redistribution of land must be made upon the most equitable basis possible, and that

---

8   The Consolidation of Agricultural Holdings in the United Provinces, 1918, pp. 45-46. The author is grateful to Prof. Jevons for a copy.

liberal compensation should be given to those, if any, who may be excluded from a former cultivating ownership."[9]

As for procedure in the compulsory consolidation of holdings both Prof. Jevons and the Baroda Committee propose the appointment of Commissioners to hear applications for consolidation and to carry it out, leaving to any objector the right to petition the Court to stay the proceedings in. case he felt that an injustice was being done to him.

The problem of perpetuating such a consolidated holding will next demand the care of the legislator. It is accepted without question by many that the law of inheritance that prevails among the Hindus and the Mohomedans is responsible for the sub-division of land. On the death of a Hindu or a Mahomedan his heirs are entitled without let or hindrance to equal shares in the property of the deceased. Now a consolidated holding subject to the operation of such a law of inheritance will certainly not endure for long. It will be the task of Sisyphus over again if, after consolidation, the law of inheritance were to remain unaltered.

---

9   Besides these two systems of inheritance there is a third which allows a father liberty to do as he likes with a part of his estate provided he leaves sufficient for his heir to constitute what is called pars legitima. Under it the Germans have enacted a permissive law of Anerbenrecht designed to obviate the effects of the law of inheritance in causing unnecessary sub-division of land. In some aspects it anticipates the proposals of the Baroda Committee; in others those of the Hon. Mr. Keatings.   For a description of it see Prof. N. G. Pierson's Principles of Economics, Vol. II, pp. 286-90.

But how is the existing law of inheritance to be changed? If it is not to be the law of equal sub-division shall we have the law of primogeniture. The Baroda Committee thanks that,—

"It is not necessary that it should be introduced. All that it wanted is, that there should not be sub-divisions of land beyond a certain limit, which may be fixed for the sake of good agriculture. There is no objection to a holding being sub-divided, so long as by so doing each of the parts does not become less than the limit fixed for the sub-division of land. But when a holding reaches a stage to render further sub-division uneconomic, the other members of the family may not be allowed to force further sub-division of the holding. Instead of being sub-divided, it may be either cultivated in common or be given to one of the members of the family as a whole, and that member made to pay amounts equal to the value of their shares as compensation to the other members."[10]

The principle of not dividing immovable property among the heirs, when division would result in inconveniently small shares, but of giving to the highest bidder among the sharers or in case none of them is willing to have it, to outside bidders, and dividing the money realized in proportion to the recognized shares, has been accepted in the Indian Partition Act, No. 4 of 1893, section 2 of which runs thus:

"Whenever in any suit for partition, in which, if instituted prior to the commencement of this Act, a decree for partition might have been made, it appears to the Court that, by reason of the nature of the property to which the suit relates, or of the number of the shareholders therein or of any other special circumstance,

---

10 R.B.C., p. 26.

a division of the property cannot reasonably or conveniently be made and that a sale of the property and distribution of proceeds would be more beneficial for all the share-holders, the Court may, if it thinks fit, on the request of any such share-holder interested individually or collectively to the extent of one moiety or upwards direct a sale of the property and a distribution of the proceeds."

Granting the advisability of thus changing the law of inheritance it only requires to amend the Civil Procedure Code so as to make it obligatory on the Courts to refuse partition whenever it would reduce a field beyond the economic limit fixed in advance.

Another method of dealing with the problem is advocated by the Hon. Mr. G. F. Keatinge, Director of Agriculture, Bombay Presidency. In the Statement of Objects and Reasons appended to his draft bill he says:

"4.................. The object of this bill is to enable such landowners as may wish to do so to check: the further sub-division of their lands and to enable them, when it is otherwise possible, to effect a permanent consolidation of their holdings; and also to enable the executive government to secure the same results in respect of unoccupied land. The legislation proposed is purely enabling, and it will be operative in the case of any holding only upon the expressed wish of any person possessing an interest in that holding.

"5. The scheme embodied in this bill for securing these objects is briefly as follows. In order to be constituted an economic holding a plot of land must be entered as such in a register prescribed by rules. If the land is occupied, it will rest with some person having an interest in the land to make an application to the Collector to have the land registered as an economic holding........... Unless the

Collector considers that there are sufficient grounds for rejecting the application, he holds a careful enquiry in which he follows a procedure similar to that prescribed in the Land Acquisition Act, 1894. If the proceedings show that all persons interested agree, the land is registered. Land vesting absolutely in Government may be registered without inquiry. The holding must in any case be registered in one name only, and the act of registration annuls all the interest of all other persons, except the registered owner, in the holding. Thereafter the owner cannot divide the plot but must so long as he owns it, keep it entire. He may sell, mortgage or otherwise dispose of it as an entire unit, but not dispose of part of it or do anything that might result in splitting up the holding. On the death of the holder, if he has not disposed of the land by will it will devolve upon a single heir. If the provisions of the bill are contravened (for instance if the holder mortgages a part of his Holding and the mortgagee obtains a decree for possession), the Collector is empowered to send a certificate to the Court, and the Court will set aside its decree or order. The Collector may also evict a person in wrongful possession. When a plot has been once constituted an economic holding, the registration cannot be cancelled except with the consent of the Collector ; the grounds on which cancellation will be allowed, will be laid down by rule and it is proposed that it shall be permitted chiefly in cases where economic considerations indicate that it is expedient."

Summing up this discussion of the two issues of consolidation, it must be said that the problem has not been viewed as a whole by all its advocates. The Baroda Committee alone endeavours to consolidate as well as to preserve the consolidated holding. Prof. Jevons makes no provision to conserve the results of consolidation. Mr. Keatinge does not deal with consolidation at all. He is concerned only with the prevention of further fragmentation. But fragmentation, there will be in a holding even after it is entered as an economic holding. By his measure he will only succeed in preserving the holdings, as they will be found at the time of registration, i.e., he will not allow them to be reduced in size. But they will be small and scattered all the same. Mr. Keatinge, notwithstanding his legislation, leaves the situation more or less as it exists. Real consolidation is, however, aimed at by Prof. Jevons and the Baroda Committee. The principles they advocate for the purpose are almost the same ; and so are their procedures for carrying it out.

As for the preservation of consolidated holdings Mr. Keatinge as well as the Baroda Committee establish the one-man rule of succession. The Baroda Committee would adopt this rule only when division of land would result in uneconomic holdings and then too would compel the successor to buy off the claims of the other dispossessed heirs. Mr. Keatinge would let the dispossessed heirs off without compensation.

A more serious criticism against these projects of consolidation consists in the fact they have failed to recognize that a consolidated holding must be an enlarged holding as well. If it is said that Indian agiculture suffers from small and scattered holdings we must not only consolidate, but also enlarge them. It must be borne in mind that consolidation may obviate the evils of scattered holdings, but it will not obviate the evils of small holdings unless the consolidated holding is an economic, i.e. an enlarged holding. The Committee as well as Mr. Keatinge have entirely lost sight of this aspect of the question. Prof. Jevons, alone of the advocates, keeps it constantly before his mind that consolidation must bring about in its train the enlargement of holdings.

IV

ENLARGEMENT

Granted that enlargement of holdings is as important as their consolidation we will now turn to the discussion of regulating their size. It is desired by all interested in our agriculture that our holdings should be economic holdings. We would have been more thankful to the inventors of this new, precise and scientific terminology had they given us a precise and scientific definition of an economic holding. On the other hand, it is believed that a large holding is somehow an economic holding. It may be said that even Prof. Jevons has fallen a victim to this notion. For when discussing what the size of a holding should be he dogmatically states that in the consolidated village the mode should be between 29 and 30 acres.[11] But why should the mode be at this point and not at 100 or say 200 ? We might imagine Pro. Jevons to reply that his model point is placed at that particular acreage because it would produce enough for a farmer to sustain a higher standard of living. Raising the general standard of living in India is the one string on which Prof. Jevons harps even to weariness throughout his pamphlet.[12] The error underlying this doctrine we shall consider later on. It is enough to say that he does not give any sound economic reason for his model farm.

---

11   Opt. Cit. chart on p. 38.

12   Opt. Cit. Introduction.

The case with the Baroda Committee is much worse, Prof. Jevons at least sticks to one definition of an ideal economic holding ; but the Report of the Baroda Committee suffers from a plurality of definitions. While cementing on the size of an average holding in the state as is summarized in the above table, it should be noted that the Committee, though it desired consolidation, was perfectly satisfied with the existing size of the holding as is clear, from the following:

"If the average holding of a Khatedar was a compact field of those figures, the situation would be an ideal one and would not leave much to be desired."[13]

But absent-minded as it were, the Committee, without any searching analysis of the question it was appointed to investigate and report upon, lays down that :

"An ideal economic holding would consist of 30 to 50 bighas of fair land in one block with at least one good irrigation well and a house situated in the holding."[14]

If the size of existing holdings is an ideal size why should they be enlarged ? To this, the Committee gives no answer. But this is not all. The Committee does not even adhere to the quantitative limit it has already set down to its ideal economic holding. When it comes to discuss the project of re-arrangement of the scattered fields of the village on the principle of " Economic unit " it presents a third ideal of an economic holding. To realize this ideal it says :

"Each of these new plots must be of such a size, as having regard to the local conditions of soil, tillage, etc., to form an Economic

---

13   Ibid., p. 4.

14   R.B.C., p. 31.

field, i.e., a parcel of land necessary to keep fully engaged and support one family."[15]

Thus with perfect equanimiy (1) the Baroda Committee holds, not too fast, to three notions of an ideal economic holding. No wonder then that the Report of the Committee is a model of confused reasoning though it is a valuable repository of facts bearing on the subject.

According to the Hon. Mr. Keatinge an economic holding is:— " a holding which allows a man chance of producing sufficient to support himself and his family in reasonable comfort, after paying his necessary expenses."[16]

His definition of an economic holding will be accepted, we may expect, by the Baroda Committee; for, it does not differ from its own, given above as third in order. Assuming they agree, we may now proceed to see how far tenable this definition is

It is plain that these definitions including that of Professor Jevons view an economic holding from the standpoint of consumption rather than of production. In this lies their error; for consumption is not the correct standard by which to judge the economic character of a holding. It would be perverse accounting to condemn a farm as not paying because its total output does not support the family of the farmer though as a pro-rata return for each of his investments it is the highest. The family of a farmer can only be looked upon in the light of so much labour corps at his disposal. It may well be that some portion of this labour corps is superfluous, though it has to be supported merely in obedience to social custom as is the case

---

15   Ibid, p. 53.
16   Rural Economy in the Bombay Deccan, p. 51.

in India. But if our social custom compels a farmer to support some of his family members even when he cannot effectively make any use of them on his farm we must be careful not to find fault with the produce of the farm because it does not suffice to provide for the workers as well as the dependants that may happen to compose the family. The adoption of such an accounting system will declare many enterprises as failures when they will be the most successful. There can be no true economic relation between the family of the entrepreneur and the total out-turn of his farm or industry. True economic relation can subsist only between the total out-turn and the investments. If the total out-turn pays for all the investments no producer in his senses will ever contemplate closing his industry because the total out-turn does not support his family. This is evident ; for though production is for the purpose of consumption it is for the consumption only of those who help to produce. It follows, then, that if the relation between out-turn and investments is a true economic relation, we can only speak of a farm as economic, i.e., paying in the sense of production and not in the sense of consumption. Any definition, therefore, that leans on consumption mistakes the nature of an economic holding which is essentially an enterprise in production.

Before going further, we must clear the ground by a few preliminary remarks to facilitate the understanding of an economic holding from the standpoint of production.

It must be premised at the outset that in a competitive society the daily transactions of its members, as consumers or producers, are controlled by a price regime. It is production, then, in a price regime that we have to analyse here for our purpose. In the main the modern process of production is captained by the entrepreneur, is guided and supervised by him and is worked out through him. All employers of labour or hirers of instrumental goods are entrepreneurs. His computations run, as they must, in a pecuniary society, in terms of price-outlay as over against price-product, no matter whether the prospective product is offered for sale or not. The entrepreneur, in producing for gain, apportions his outlays in varieties of investments, These investments, the same as factors of production or costs to the entrepreneur, have by tradition been confined to wages (labour) profits, rent (land) and interest (capital). Industrial facts do not support this classification. There are many other factors, it is contended, which as they share in the distributive process must have functioned in the productive process, in some way immediate or remote. But it is immaterial how many factors there are and whether they differ in kind or degree. What is important for the purpose of production is the process of combining them.

This combination of necessary factors of production is governed by a law called the law of proportion. It lays down that disadvantage is bound to attend upon a wrong proportion among the various factors of production employed in a concern. Enlarged, the principle means that as a certain volume of one factor has the capacity to work only with a certain volume of another to give maximum efficiency to both, an excess or defect in the volume of one in comparison with those of the others will tell on the total output by curtailing the efficiency of all. Having regard then to this interdependence of factors, an economically efficient combination of them compels the producer if he were to vary the one to vary the rest correspondingly. Neither can it be otherwise. For, the chief object of an efficient production consists in making every factor in the concern contribute its highest ; and it can do that only when it can co-operate with its fellow of the required capacity. Thus, there is an ideal of proportions that ought to subsist among the various factors combined, though the ideal will vary with the changes in the proportions.[17]

These proportions it must be acknowledged are affected by the principle of substitution chiefly brought into play owing to variations in the prices of the factors. But this principle of substitution is too limited in its application to invalidate the law of proportion which is the law governing all economic production and which no producer can hope to ignore with impunity.[18]

Bringing to bear the above remarks regarding production on the definition of an economic holding, we can postulate that if agricul-

---

17　This description of the process of production is pieced together from the remarks of Prof. H. J. Davenport in his masterly treatise "The Economics of Enterprize" New York. Macmillan, 1913, In this connection see also the able paper by Prof. Henry C. Taylor on "Two Dimensions of Productivity" read before the 29th Annual Meeting of the American Economic Association held in December 1916 and the remarks on the same by Prof. A. A. Young. Both these will be found in the American Economic Review for March 1917.

18　Some economists who hold that it is the law of Diminishing Returns that governs agricultural production will demur to the universal applicability that is claimed for the Law of Proportion. Briefly stated the Law of Diminishing Returns asserts that additional 'doses' of capital and labour administered to a given piece of land will be responded to by a less and less yield. This means that if only the non-land expense of production is doubled there results less than a doubled product. But if this is the fact that is intended to be generallised by the Law of Diminishing Returns then there is nothing in it that

ture is to be treated as an economic enterprise, then, by itself, there could be no such thing as a large or a small holding. To a farmer a holding is too small or too large for the other factors of production at his disposal necessary for carrying on the cultivation of his holding as an economic enterprise. Mere size of land is empty of all economic connotation. Consequently, it cannot possibly be the language of economic science to say that a large holding is economic while a smallholding is uneconomic. It is the right or wrong proportion of other factors of production to a unit of land that renders the latter economic or uneconomic. Thus a small farm may be economic as well as a large farm; for, economic or uneconomic does not depend upon the size of land but upon the due proportion among all the factors including land.

An economic holding, therefore, if it. is not to be a hollow concept, consists in a combination of land, capital and labour, etc., in a proportion such that the pro rata contribution of each in conjunction with the rest is the highest. In other words to create an economic holding it will not do for a farmer solely to manipulate his piece of land. He must also have the other instruments of production required for the efficient cultivation of his holding and must maintain a due proportion of all the factors for, without it, there can be no efficient production. If his equipment shrinks, his holding must also shrink. If his equipment augments, his holding must also augment. The point is that his equipment and his holding

is peculiar to agricultural production. It the expense to the land be doubled but the land not doubled it is certain that the extra return will fall short of the increased expense. This is simply another way of saying that if the returns are to grow all the factors must be increased in proportion. But so stated is not the Law of Diminishing Returns a confused version of the Law of Proportion?

must not be out of proportion to each other. They must be in proportion and must vary, if need be, in proportion.

The line of argument followed above is not without support from actual practice. It is happy from an economist's point of view, to find it recognized and adopted in India itself by the fathers of the Survey and Settlement System in the Bombay Presidency. The famous Joint Report (1840) contains an illuminating discussion of the problem. The question before the officers deputed to introduce the Survey System in the Deccan was how to levy the assessment. Was it to be a field assessment or an assessment to be placed on the whole lands of the village or on the entire holdings of individuals or co-parceners, whether proprietors or occupants. That after much deliberation the system of field assessment was finally adopted is known to many. But as the reasons that led to its adoption are known only to a few the following explanatory parts from the Joint report will be found to be both interesting and instructive:

"Para 6. That one manifest advantage of breaking up the assessment of a village into portions so minute [as indicated by a survey number] is the facility it affords to the cultivators of contracting or enlarging his farm from year to year, according to the fluctuating amount of agricultural capital at their disposal which is of incalculable importance to farmers possessed of so limited resources as those of the cultivating classes throughout India.

"Para 7. The loss of a few bullocks by disease or other causes may quite incapacitate a ryot from cultivating profitably the extent of land he had previously in village and, without the privilege of contracting his farm, and consequent liabilities on occasion of such loss, his ruin would be very shortly consummated."[19]

Judging in the light of this conclusion the proposal to regulate the size of holdings appears ill considered and futile. For as Prof. Richard T. Ely observes:[20]

" Obviously no simple answer can be given to the question [as to what should be the size of a farm]. The value of land or the rent it will bring is perhaps the most important factor........................ In addition to the factor of rent the amount of capital that he can command, the kind of farming in which he is most skilled, the character of the labour he can secure, the proximity of markets, and the adequacy of transportation facilities, all must be taken into account by the farmer in determining how large a farm he will attempt to manage and how intensively he will farm it.

" This question is primarily one of private profit which the individual must decide far himself, but the legislator and the scientific student can be of some assistance in helping to develop that most difficult branch of commercial science—farm accounting—and in keeping the farmer alive to those charges in prices, wages, and transportation charges to which the farm organization must adjust itself."

To those who have the temerity to fix the size of a holding Prof. Ely's well-considered opinion will bring home that in spite of good intentions their vicarious mission will end in disaster ; for none but the cultivator can decide what should be the size of his holding. They would do well to remember that the size of his holdings will

---

19   Survey Settlement Manual Bombay Presidency, 1882. p. 3.

20   Outlines of Economics, pp. 531-32 (Italics ours).

vary in time. Consequent to the changes in his equipment with which he has to adjust the size of his farm, at one point in time he will decide in favour of a small, as at another he will decide in favour of a large holding. He would therefore be a poor economist who would legally fix the size of the holding which in the interest of economic production must be left to vary when variation is demanded. By fixing the size of a holding he can only make it a large holding but not an economic holding. For an economic holding is not a matter of the size of land alone but is a matter of the adjustment of a piece of land to the necessary equipment for its efficient cultivation.

V

CRITIQUE OF THE REMEDIES

The proposal to enlarge the existing holdings which is brought forward as a cure to the ills of our agriculture can be entertained only if it is shown that farms have diminished in size while the agricultural stock has increased in amount. Facts regarding the size of farms have already been recorded. It only remains to see if the agricultural stock has increased. Mr. K. L. Datta in his exhaustive survey says:[21]

"178. Most of the Indian witnesses, whom we examined, appeared to be under the belief that there has been a decrease in the supply of agricultural products, owing to the inefficient tillage of land. It was said that land is not now cultivated as carefully and efficiently as before, owing to the scarcity and dearness of plough, cattle and labour. In order to effect, a saving in the cost of cultivation, cultivators do not also plough their lands as often as they did before, and manuring and weeding, as also the amount of irrigating where wells are used for the purpose, have all been reduced."

"179. As regards the scarcity of plough cattle... (the) figures bear testimony to the deplorable effects of famine, the inevitable result of which has always been to reduce the number of cattle, though the deficiency is generally made good in a few years if otherwise favourable. The number of plough cattle in the latest year (1908-

---

21 Report on the Enquiry into the Rise of Prices in India, 1914, Vol. I, pp. 66-67, (Italics ours).

09) included in the statement was lower than in the commencement (1893-94), in some of the circles namely Assam, Bundelkhund, Agra Provinces—North and West, Gujarat, Deccan, Berar, Madras-North and Madras-West. Although great reliance cannot be placed on these statistics, they can be accepted as showing that in some areas at any rate there has been a dearth of plough cattle."

Regarding the existence of capital Mr. Elliot James says:

"The ryots have a keen eye to the results of a good system of farming as exhibited on model farms, but they cannot derive much good from the knowledge though they may take it in and thoroughly understand that superior tillage and proper manuring mean a greater outturn in crops. Their great want is capital"[22]

The farmer knows, says the same author, that his agricultural equipment is inefficient and antiquated but he cannot substitute better ones in its place for:

"A superior class of cattle and superior farm implements mean to him so much outlay of what he has not—Money."

Similar facts for the Baroda State have been collected in another connection by Mr. M. B. Nanavati, Director of Commerce and Indus. But unfortunately he did not bring his knowledge of such facts to bear upon the conclusions of the Committee for the consolidation of holdings in the State of which he was also a member, apparently thinking that the size of a holding bore no relation to the instruments of production. He bemoans that:

"The farmers are not fully equipped with draught-cattle. They have today (1913) 8,34,901 bullocks, etc., for use on farms, that

22   Indian Industries, p. 6.

is one pair for 36 bighas of land. On an average a pair of good bullocks can cultivate 25 bighas of land. But the present breed has much deteriorated and one pair is supposed to cultivate 20 bighas at the most, while the present actual averages comes to about 36 bighas. Under the circumstances it is not likely that ploughing can be deep. It must be like scratching the surface. The small cultivators do not possess any draught-cattle or at the most a single one and cultivate land in co-operation with their friends similarly situated. As for farm implements there are 1,54,364 ploughs in the State, i.e., one for two Khatedars. It must be understood here that the number of cultivators and tenants is much more than three lakhs- Every one of them needs full equipment. Therefore actually the average must be much smaller than shown above."[23]

In fact the equipment for agricultural production in the State has considerably deteriorated since 1898 as shown by the table below :

Year	Plough	Carts	Plough Cattle	Other Domestics
1898	1,75,989	---	4,15,089	5,70,517
1910	1,51,664	68,946	3,34,801	5,09,416

Given, this state of affairs can we not say with more propriety that not only the existing equipment is inadequate for the enlarged holdings but that the existing holdings, small as they are, are too big for the available instruments of production other than land? Facts such as these interpreted in the light of our theory force upon us the conclusion that the existing holdings are uneconomic, not, however, in the sense that they are too small but that they are too

---

23 Report on Agricultural Indebtedness in the Baroda State, 1913, para. 35.

large. Shall we therefore argue that the existing holdings should be further reduced in size with a view to render them economic in the sense in which we have used the term ? Unwary readers might suppose that this is the -only logical and inevitable conclusion— a conclusion that is in strange contrast with the main trend of opinion in) this country. Contrary, no doubt, the conclusion is ; but it is by no means inevitable. For, from our premises we can with perfect logic and even with more cogency argue for increase in agricultural stock and implements which in turn will necessitate enlarged holdings which will be economic holdings as well.

Consequently the remedy for the ills of agriculture in India does not lie primarily in the matter of enlarging holdings but in the matter of increasing capital and capital goods. That capital arises from saving and that saving is possible where there is surplus is a commonplace of political economy.

Does our agriculture—the main stay of our population—-give us any surplus ? We agree with the answer which is unanimously in the negative. We also approve of the remedies that are advocated for turning the deficit economy into a surplus economy, namely by enlarging and consolidating the holdings. What we demur to is the method of realizing this object. For we most strongly hold that the evil of small holdings in India is not fundamental but is derived from the parent evil of the mal-adjustment in her social economy. Consequently if we wish to effect a permanent cure we must go to the parent malady.

But before doing that we will show how we suffer by a bad social economy. It has become a tried statement that India is largely an agricultural country. But what is scarcely known is that notwithstanding the vastness of land under tillage, so little land is cultivated in proportion to her population.

Mulhall's figures for the year 1895 clearly demonstrate the point. Acres per inhabitant in 1895

Great Britain	Ireland	France	Germany	Russia	Austria	Italy	Spain And Portugal	USA	India
0.91	3.30	2.30	1.70	5.60	2.05	1.75	2.90	8.90	1.0

That since 1895 the situation, however, has gone from bad to worse figures eloquently bear out :

	1881	1891	1901	1911
Bengal	1.5	0.8	1.12	
Bombay	1.7	1.6	1.41	1.3
Madras	1.3	0.3	.68	.79
Assam		0.5	.78	.85
Punjab	1.2	1.3	1.05	1.11
Oudh	0.81	0.7}		.75
N. W. P.	-	0.8}	.73	
Burmah	-	1.5	1	1.09
Central P	1.67	2.4	1.8	1.79
B. India	1.04	1.0	0.86	0.88

Now, what does this extraordinary phenomenon mean? A large agricultural population with the lowest proportion of land in actual cultivation means that a large part of the agricultural population is superfluous and idle. How much idle labour there is on, Indian farms it is not possible to know accurately. Sir James Caird who was the first to notice the existence of this idle labour estimated in 1884 that,

"A square mile of land in England cultivated highly gives employment to 50 persons, in the proportion 25 men, young and old, and 25 women and boys. If four times that number, or 200, were allowed for each square mile of cultivated land in India, it would take up only one-third of the population."[24]

Out of the total population of 254 millions in 1881 nearly two-thirds were returned as agricultural. Allowing, as per estimate, one-third to be taken up, we can safely say that a population of equal magnitude was lying idle instead of performing any sort of productive labour. With the increasing ruralization of India and a continually decreasing proportion of land under cultivation, the volume of idle labour must have increased to an enormous extent.

The economic effects of this idle labour are two-fold. Firstly, it adds to the tremendous amount of pressure that our agricultural population exerts on land. A quantitative statement will serve to bring home to our mind how high the pressure is:

---

24   India, the Land and the People, p. 225.

Mean density per square mile in 1911

	Oudh and N.W.P.	Bengal	Madras	Punjab	Bombay	Assam	Berar and C.P	Coorg	British Burma
of Total Area of	427 829	551	291	177	145	115	122	111	53
Cultivated		1162	785					792	
				453	444	766	360		575
Area									
Area Area									

Such high pressure of population on land is probably unknown in any other part of the world. The effect of it is, of course, obvious.

Notwithstanding what others have said, this enormous pressure is the chief cause of the subdivision of land. It is the failure to grasp the working of this pressure on land that makes the law of inheritance such a great grievance. To say that the law of inheritance causes sub-division of land is to give a false view by inverting the real situation. The mere existence of the law cannot be complained of as a grievance. The grievance consists in the fact that it is invoked. But why is it invoked even when it is injurious ? Simply because it is profitable. There is nothing strange in this. When farming is the only occupation, to get a small piece of land is better than to have none. Thus the grievance lies in the circumstances which put a premium on these small pieces of land. The premium, is no doubt, due to the large population depending solely on agriculture to eke out its living. Naturally a population that has little else lo prefer to agriculture will try lo invoke every possible cause to get a piece of land however small. It is not therefore the law of inheritance that is the evil, but it is the high pressure on land which brings it into operation. People cultivate the small piece not because their standard of living is low as Prof. Jevons seems to think[25] but because it is the only profitable thing for them to do at

---

25 Opt. cit. Introduction. The Impression that Prof. Jevons leaves on his readers is that agriculture suffers in India because of the low standard of living. That a higher standard of life once established will necessitate a large holding because people with a high standard of life will prefer to migrate rather than accept a small holding. As his argument that holdings and standard of life are related is likely to mislead his less thoughtful readers, a word of comment is necessary. A standard of living is merely a level of consumption fixed in habit. But what determines

present. If they had something more profitable to do they would never prefer the small piece. It is therefore easy to understand how the universal prevalence of the small farms or petit culture is due to this enormous pressure on land.

In spite of the vehement struggle that our agricultural population maintains in trying to engage itself productively as cultivators of a farm however small, it is true that judged by the standard of Sir James Caird a large portion of it is bound to remain idle. Idle labour and idle capital differ in a very important particular. Capital exists, but labour lives. That is to say capital when idle does not earn, but does not also consume much to keep itself. But labour, earning or not consumes in order to live. Idle labour is, therefore, a calamity; for if it cannot live by production as it should, it will live by predation as it must. This idle labour has been the canker of India gnawing at its vitals. Instead of contributing to our national

---

the depth of a particular level of consumption? Undoubtedly the level of production. We may grant the truth of the statement that a rise in the standard of living works as a stimulus to higher production but it is foolish to expect mere wish to be father to the deed. It is actual production alone that can support rise in the standard and not wish, generated though it be either by "travel or education". If Prof. Jevons means that an opportunity for increased production, leading to a higher standard of life, will disfavour small holdings we are one with him. But he can make himself more intelligible by dropping standard of living and only arguing for increased production; that increased production leads to a rise in standard will be granted by all; but the reverse cannot be maintained Prof. Jevons seems to do, for it may lead to production or predation. To speak of raising the standard of life without speaking of increased production is to give expression to a pious wish, if it does not lead to mischief.

dividend it is eating up what little there is of it. Thus the depression of our national dividend is another important effect of this idle labour. The income of a society as of an individual proceeds (1) from the efforts made, and (2) from possessions used. It may be safely asserted that the aggregate income of any individual or society must be derived either from the proceeds of the current labour or from productive possession already acquired. All that society can have today it must acquire today or must take out of its past product. Judging by this criterion a large portion of our society makes very little current effort ; nor does it have any very extensive possessions from which to derive its sustenance. No doubt then that our economic organization is conspicuous by want of capital. Capital is but crystallized surplus; and surplus depends upon the proceeds of effort. But where there is no effort there is no earning, no surplus, and no capital.

We have thus shown how our bad social economy is responsible for the ills of our agriculture. We have also proved how our entire dependence on agriculture leads to small and scattered farms. How a large portion of our population which our agriculture cannot productively employ is obliged to remain idle has been made clear. We have also shown how the existence of this idle labour makes ours a country without capital. This being our analysis of the problem, it will be easy to see why the remedies for consolidation and enlargement under the existing social economy arc bound to fail.

Those who look on small holdings as the fundamental evil naturally advocate their enlargement. This, however, is a faulty political economy and as Thomas Arnold once said "a faulty political economy is the fruitful parent of crime". Apart from the fact that merely to enlarge the holding is not to make it economic, this project of artificial enlargement is fraught with many social ills. The future in the shape of an army of landless and dispossessed men that it is bound to give rise to is neither cheerful from the individual, nor agreeable from the national, point of view. But even if we enlarged the existing holdings and procured enough capital and capital goods to make them economic, we will not only be not advocating the proper remedy but will end in aggravating the evils by adding to our stock of idle labour ; for capitalistic agriculture will not need as many hands as are now required by our present day methods of cultivation.

But if enlargement is not possible, can we not have consolidation? It can be shown that under the existing social economy even consolidation is not possible. The remedy for preventing sub-division and fragmentation of consolidated holdings cannot be expected to bring real relief. Instead it will only serve to be a legal eyewash. This becomes easy of comprehension if we realize at the start what the one man rule of succession means in actual practice. For this we shall have to note the changes it will introduce in the survey records. At present according to the Bombay Land Revenue Code Chapter I, Section 3, clause (6).

"Survey Number" means a portion of land of which the area and other particulars are separately entered, under an indicative number in the survey records of the village, town or city in which it is situated, and includes a recognized share of a survey number. Again by clause (7).

" Recognized share of a survey number " means a sub-division of a survey number separately assessed and registered.

After the adoption of the one man rule of succession a survey number will be made to cover a piece of land which will be of the size fixed for an ideal economic holding. Secondly, it will be necessary to refuse separate registration to any sub-division of such a survey number; i.e., in order that a piece of land should be registered with a separate and a distinct survey number it must not be below the economic limit. Then too this survey number covering a piece of land large enough to be styled economic will be registered in the name of one person. This is precisely what will happen if we put into practice the project of the Baroda Committee. Mr. Keatinge instead of having one survey number covering a large and compact holding will have in the name of one person many survey numbers covering a unit of land composed of small and scattered fields. Abandoning Mr. Keatinge's scheme as serving no practical purpose the one man rule of succession lo a consolidated holding means in practice refusal to recognize legally a piece of land if it were below a certain size. Now this refusal to recognize smaller pieces of land, it is claimed, will prevent the sub-division of a consolidated holding: Sub-division of land may be due to many causes the operation of which is rendered economic or uneconomic by the nature of the occasion which evokes it. Not to allow sub-division on any ground, as does Mr. Keatinge, is to cause a serious depreciation of the value of land. But if sub-division is needed as when the stock has depleted, not to grant it is to create an uneconomic situation—a result just opposite of what is intended to be achieved, apart from this to prevent sub-division legally is not to prevent it actually, if necessitated by the weight of economic circumstances.

Granting the pressure of population on land and the scanty agricultural equipment—evils to which the authors of consolidation and enlargement have paid no attention—we must look forward to the sub-division of holdings. If we legislate in the face of this inevitable tendency and refuse to record on our survey roll holdings below a certain limit required for a separate survey number we will not only fail to cure what we must know we cannot, at least by this means, but will help to create a register that will be false to the true situation.

This being our criticism of the means for preventing sub-division and fragmentation it will not take us long to state our view as regards the project of consolidation. Consolidation and its conservation are so intimately connected that the one cannot be thought of without the other. Now if we cannot conserve a consolidated holding, is it worth our while to consolidate, however feasible the project may be? This work of Sysiphus will not fail to fall to our lot unless we make effective changes in our social economy.

As the evils of this surplus and idle labour which will be added on to by the consolidation and enlargement of holdings are likely to outweigh their advantages, the proposals do not find much favour at the hands of Prof. Gilbert Slater.[26]

As against Prof. Slater we hold that the evils are avoidable and it is because we are anxious to avoid them that we wish to advocate different remedies for bringing about the enlargement of holdings.

---

26   "The village in the Melting Pot" Journal of the Indian Economic Society. Vol. 1. No. I, p. 10.

Consequently, we maintain that our efforts should be primarily directed towards this idle labour.[27]

If we succeed in sponging off this labour in non-agricultural channels of production we will at one stroke lessen the pressure and destroy the premium that at present weighs heavily on land in India. Besides, this labour when productively employed will cease to live by predation as it does to-day, and will not only earn its keep but will give us surplus: and more surplus is more capital. In short, strange though it may seem, industrialization of India is the soundest remedy for the agricultural problems of India. The cumulative effects of industralization, namely, a lessening pressure and an increasing amount of capital and capital goods will forcibly create the economic necessity of enlarging the holding. Not only this, but industralization by destroying the premium on land will give rise to few occasions for its sub-division and fragmentation. Industrialization is a natural and powerful remedy and is to be pre-

---

27 Prof. Jevons does speak of removing the surplus agricultural population to towns. The author is happy to note that Prof. Jevons had recognised that there is the evil of surplus population. What he has failed to recognize is that this evil is the faithful parent of all other evils that affect our agriculture. When it is recalled that industrialization of India is the one theme against which Prof. Jevons never fails to argue with all the aid of his knowledge and influence, his remedy of removing the surplus population to towns sounds starnge; for migration to towns is simply euphemism for the industrialization of India. On the other hand Prof. Jevons has forgotten that there are few towns in India. If we believe, as does Prof. Jevons, that there is the evil of surplus population the only logical and inevitable conclusion, however unplatable it be, is the creations of more towns i.e. industrialization.

ferred to such ill-conceived projects as we have considered above. By legislation we will get a sham economic holding at the cost of many social ills. But by industrialization a large economic holding will force itself upon us as a pure gain.

Our remedy for the enlargement as for the consolidation of holdings as well as the preservation of consolidated holdings reduces itself to this: We prefer to cure agriculture by the reflex effects of industrialization. Lest this might be deemed visionary we proceed to give evidence in support of our view. How agriculture improves by the reflex effects of industrialization has been studied in the United States in the year 1883. We shall quote in extenso the summary given by the London Times:

"The statistician of the Agricultural Department of the United States has shown in a recent report that the value of farm lands decreases in exact proportion as the ratio of agriculture to other industries increases. That is, where all the labour is devoted to agriculture, the land is worth less than where only half of the people are farm labourers; and where only a quarter of them are so engaged the farms and their product are still more valuable. It is, in fact, proved by statistics that diversified industries are of the greatest value to a State, and that the presence of a manufactory near a farm increases the value of the farm and its crops. It is further established that, dividing the United States into four sections or classes, with reference to the ratio of agricultural workers to the whole population, and putting those States having less than 30 per cent, of agriculture and of agricultural labourers in the first class, all having over 30 and less than 50 in the second, those between 50 and 70 in the third, and those having 70 or more in the fourth, the value of farms is in inverse ratio to the agricultural population, and that where as in the purely agricultural section, the fourth class, the value of farms per acre is only \$ 5.28, in the next class it is \$ 13.03, in the third \$ 22.21, and in   manufacturing districts \$ 40.91. This shows an enormous advantage for a mixed district. Yet not only is the land more valuable the production per acre is greater, and the wages paid to farm hands larger. Manufactures and varied industries thus not only benefit the manufacturers, but are of equal benefit and advantage to the fanners as well."

This will show that ours is a proven remedy. It can be laid down without fear of challenge that industrialization will foster the enlargement of holdings and that it will be the most effective barrier against sub-division and fragmentation. Agreeing in this, it may be observed that industrialization will not be a sufficient remedy for consolidation. That it will require direct remedies may be true. But it is also true that industrialization, though it may not bring about consolidation, will facilitate consolidation. It is an incontrovertible truth that so long as there is the premium on land consolidation will not be easy, no matter on how equitable principles it is proposed to be carried out. Is it a small service if industrialization lessens the premium as it inevitably must ? Certainly not. Consideration of another aspect of consolidation as well points to the same conclusion: That industrialization must precede consolidation. It should never be forgotten that unless we have constructed an effective barrier against the future sub-division and fragmentation of a consolidated holding it is idle to lay out plans for consolidation. Such a barrier can only be found in industrialization ; for it alone can reduce the extreme pressure which, as we have shown, causes sub-division of land. Thus. if small and scattered holdings are the

ills from which our agriculture is suffering to cure it of them is un-
deniably to industrialize.

But just where does India stand as an industrial country?:

	England and Wales		Germany		USA		France		India	
	Rural	Urban	Rural	Urban	Rural	Urban	Rural	Urban	Rural	Urban
1790					87.5					
1840					77.5		75.6	24.4		
1851	49.92	50.08								
1871	38.20	61.80		36	47.6					
1881	32.1	67.9		41	44.3	29.5				
1891	27-95	72.05		47	39.2	36.1			64.4	
1901	23-00	77.00		54	35.7	40.5			67.5	
1911	19-9	78.1			33.3	46.3	57.9	42.1	71.5	

(The figures for the various countries do not correspond with
the years. The range of variation is 3 years).

Sir Robert Giffen after a survey of the economic tendencies of
various countries concludes that.

"The wants of men increasing with their resources the proportion of people engaged in agriculture and mining and analogous
pursuits, in every country is destined to decline, and that of people
engaged in miscellaneous industry—in. other words in manufactures using the latter phrase in a wide sense to increase."[28]

Figures for India, however, run counter to this dictum illustrating
a universal tendency observed by an expert. While other countries

28 Essays in Finance" 2nd Series, p. 240.

like the U.S.A. starting as agricultural are progressively becoming industrial, India has been gradually undergoing the woeful process of de-urbanization and swelling the volume of her rural population beyond all needs. The earlier we stem this ominous tide, the better. For notwithstanding what interested persons might say[29] no truer and more wholesome words of caution were ever uttered regarding our national economy than those by Sir Henry Cotton when he said **"There is danger of too much agriculture in India."**

29　Prof. Jevons in his paper on the "Capitalistic Development of Agriculture" read before the Indian Industrial Conference, held at Bombay in December 1915 argues against industrialisation. It can however be maintained against Prof. Jevons that it is industrialisation only that can make capitalistic agriculture possible. As a needful corrective to his paper cf. Sir Robert Giffen's Essay IV in his Essays in Finance, 1st Series.

FROM THE AUTHOR

This short story is the first in the series of short stories I named "The Last Chord". Saying more here would spoil your enjoyment and would be equal to judging a book by its cover.

All I can do is invite you, my dear reader, to follow closely the disturbances of described events and watch how they affect the heroes of these series. Put yourself in their place and see how would you react in the same situation...

Although this story is meant to be read in comfort, I would suggest removing your mind from the comfortable environment and putting yourself in the metaphorical shoes of the protagonists. I say metaphorical because all of them have three legs. Not all together – each of them has three legs, mind you. The rest of the facts you will have to find out on your own, my dear reader.